DOWN ON THE FARM

Frances T. Vena

American Literary Press, Inc.
Baltimore, Maryland

DOWN ON THE FARM

Copyright © 1999 *Frances T. Vena*

Library of Congress
Cataloging in Publication Data
ISBN 1-56167-463-X

Published by

American Literary Press, Inc.
8019 Belair Road, Suite 10
Baltimore, Maryland 21236

Manufactured in the United States of America

This novel is dedicated to my sisters and brothers and is written about our experiences of life growing up on the farm.

It is essentially written in a colloquial style– country life at its best.

Original names of people and places have been used and it is a brief sketch of towns that exist in the Lake Elsinore Valley in southern California.

CHAPTER I

THE RANCH HOUSE

There were six of us kids and what one of us couldn't think of the next one would. It must have been a riot for anyone to watch all of the monkeyshines going on. Although I don't think that anyone could outdo the pranks of the two older boys when they were growing up. With a large farm, a big two-story house and all that open space, we were more like the *Wild Bunch*.

Mom kept as watchful an eye on us as she could, but that was a large family to keep in tow—with the farm yard, a garden, the house and all that cooking. The cooking was magnified at harvest time as she always had a hot lunch for the harvesters. And then friends and relatives always chose weekends to visit the ranch where they knew they would find dinner at the large oak table in the dining room, usually chicken with mashed potatoes or macaroni and cheese. Of course there were always fresh vegetables from the garden. These were followed by a rich dessert made from all the fresh cream and butter on hand, thanks to a cow or two, and lots of eggs from all those chickens.

As if there wasn't enough cooking there would occasionally be a "man-of-the-road" stopping in for a hand out. One of these individuals had chalked a large "X" on one of the palm trees of the two rows leading up to the house from the highway. This seemed to be a sign for any so called "hobo" that he could expect a big plate of food to fill an empty stomach.

It was not unusual for them to offer a helping hand, such as cutting wood for the stove or some other task to compensate for a good meal

Ours was a large two-story frame house with four bedrooms, a sleeping porch, and one upstairs bathroom on the top floor. At first before we had electricity and the hot water heater, anyone wanting a bath had to haul up from the kitchen below a bucket or two of hot water that was heated on a large wood cooking stove.

When we were still little, Mom would either bathe us in the kitchen sink or else in the tub on the back porch so she could scrub the day's dirt off.

Downstairs consisted of a large kitchen with a kitchenette and a pantry off that, as well as a large screened porch for doing the laundry with a tub and a scrub board-before the washing machine that is. There was also a small toilet cubicle with one of those "pull-the-chain" deals. Needless to say, this and the upstairs bathroom were busy places.

The pantry not only stored dishes and canned foods in cupboards on one side but also an open shelf above low drawers on the other that held large enameled pans for holding the day's milk. The day's milk was held in these pans for two days and then skimmed of their cream that formed on the top and then deposited into a large butter chum that we two older girls would take turns at churning into butter.

The skimmed milk would often be soured in the summertime and would end up in the old pans outside for the turkeys (the dumbest things that God ever created). They literally devoured the stuff Another time, for a display of the turkey's frenzy, was when we kids picked off the green tomato worms from the garden just beyond and tossed out to watch those crazy things fight over them.

The house also had three large front rooms—the dining room, a large living room with a wood stove to keep warm in the winter, and a large entrance hall.

Now, six kids, a mother and a father weren't the only inhabitants of the house for there were two or three swarms of bees living within those wooden walls. These Papa was never able to get rid of. Several bee men had also tried and had given up.

It wasn't bad in the wintertime, but the summers were something else, especially when it was unbearably hot. Then, a few bees would invariably find a way out into the entrance hall downstairs. That was a time to keep a fly swatter on hand.

As for playing outside, the bees and we kids all rather ignored each other. If by chance we did get stung, we did as mom had told us and would scratch out the stinger and cover the bite with a little glob of mud. As the mud dried, it would draw out any poison—at least this worked for us.

We were lucky to have running water and electricity. Before electrical lines were strung down the valley, our power was generated by rows of batteries on shelves in what we called the old gas house out in the backyard.

As for the water, it was piped up from the windmill to a large tank perched on a sturdy wooden frame on a slight hill in the cow's pasture. That old windmill could really spin as we always had an afternoon wind blowing up the valley. The water would gush out into the tank and before long would overflow down the sides of the tank, making an ideal place to cool off when the summer became unbearably hot. Of course we had instructions to turn off the windmill when it ran over, but we would often manage a delaying action.

The farm was situated in a long valley in Southern California below a town called Lake Elsinore. I heard that it had derived its name from an early Mexican visitor who had so dubbed it by the smell of sulfur springs in the area, saying, "It smells like hell, senor."

The valley extended south to three small communities. Ours was the first in line and had been named Wildomar (they say it was named by an early settler after his three children: William, Dorothy, and Margaret).

The next town below ours was called Murietta. There was a small tourist spa off to one side where visitors could go to enjoy the hot sulfur springs, believing them to be beneficial and with healing powers for their rheumatism and other ailments.

The third town was called Temecula. It was an early Indian site and was the setting for the novel by Helen Hunt Jackson named *Ramona,* a story that is romanticized on a yearly basis in San Jacinto, a town east of there that had also been included in the book.

The valley was bordered by the Coast Range of mountains to the west and a low lying range of hills to the east.

Our farm, as were most of those in the valley, was strictly on a dry farming basis. Our crops ranged from alfalfa hay to that of oats and barley for animal fodder. In the autumn there was harvesting for seed: alfalfa, oats, and wheat. Depending on the rains, we would have either one or two crops of alfalfa hay. Weather fronts would blow up from Mexico or from the west. These provided the necessary rains for dry fanning.

The farming acreage was large, and with the help of a garden, chickens, eggs, and a cow or two, it was a good and healthy living for our large family. Then, there was always the sale of the crops to help fill the coffers.

The Ranch House with Dad sporting a new car.

CHAPTER II

THE WILD BUNCH

With the large farm and open space, I reiterate we were more like the *Wild Bunch*. There were three boys and three of us girls, and sometimes an occasional cousin or two as well. The two older boys, Horace and Art, were our half brothers and were a bit older than the rest of us. Our youngest brother must have been an afterthought so to speak and was not old enough for the farm chores until the older two were about ready to "fly the coop."

Our older brother, Horace, and his brother Art had their chores outside, such as feeding the cows and horses, milking the cows, chopping wood, cleaning the chicken coop and chopping off the heads of a chicken or two for the evening meal. Later, as they grew older, they were put to work in the fields to help with the harvest.

I remember once that Mom told Art to chop off the head of a chicken that he had stuck in a small coop, but he forgot. She had heated a large bucket of water on the kitchen stove to pluck the feathers. A couple of dunks in this and it was easy to get the feathers off—that wasn't new to me, but chopping off a head sure was.

I thought, "Well, if the boys can do it, I guess that I can." I grabbed the chicken by its legs in one hand, and with the axe in the other, I laid the chicken out on a log as I had seen Art do and raised the axe, but I just couldn't look, so I closed my eyes and swung the axe. To my horror, I saw that I had only cut part way through the neck and that the old biddy had slipped off the log and was running around in circles until it finally dropped dead. That was the last time I ever tried to chop a head off a chicken—someone else would have to do that job from now on.

We three girls had our chores as well. They consisted of gathering the eggs, feeding the chickens, setting the table, doing the dishes, and helping to clean the house.

We all took our turn at washing dishes while the other two did the wiping. Mary always had an excuse that she had to go to the bathroom after dinner. Evy and I soon decided that if she was going to skip out on us like that that she would have to do the work all by herself. After that she managed quite well at delaying the bathroom bit.

Spring was always a most delightful time. There were always wild flowers to pick. The fields close to the mountains in front and in back of the house would be full of poppies, our state flower, and there were the mushrooms coming up under the trees, especially some huge ones that grew under the eucalyptus trees at the end of the cows' pasture. These Mom would peel and cook in butter. Boy, were they ever good.

Once some friends that played cards with our folks stopped by the house to show us a bunch of mushrooms that they had just picked. It's a good thing that they had wanted to show them to us, for all those nice "mushrooms" were poisonous toadstools.

Our folks would play a couple tables of bridge once a week with a group of friends. It's a good thing that their friends had stopped to show off those "mushrooms" or their group would have been short two of their players. Now, I felt sorry for the player that would end up with Mom as a partner. She couldn't care less for her bridge game. She just enjoyed the company. On the other hand, Dad was a very good player, most avid when it came to cards. I was the only one that would play cards or cribbage with him as he was a stern teacher.

Those two older boys were a riot. They had fertile minds when it came to mischief. Some of their escapades were more than just mischief. I think that they must have had a guardian angel on their shoulders to survive their shenanigans.

To state a few: There was the time that they decided to give the hens a 'hot foot," so to speak. It must have been after their chore of cleaning the chicken coop, which was no picnic. They waited until after dark when the chickens had settled down for the night. Then, they went out with some matches and a flashlight where they proceeded to set fire to the tail feathers of those on the outer roost of the chicken coop. Those biddies went berserk and were flapping all over the hen house. At least they stirred up such a commotion that they managed to put their own fire out, but there were several bare bottomed chickens running around the farm after that one.

Then, there was the time that the folks and we girls headed for town to do the week's shopping, leaving Art and Horace to clean up the yard. After chasing three or four chickens out that had flown over the fence for better pickings, they decided to get even with those feathered fowls, so they got out the shotgun and sat in the gateway of the yard and took turns at knocking off those hens down in the olive orchard on one side of the house where they were always pecking at the fallen olives. After they had nailed about four or five, they gathered them up and hauled them up the far ditch and dumped them. Those olive trees were large oil olives, and sometimes a crew would come by and harvest them for their oil. They would spread large canvases under the trees and shake them with long poles.

The next morning, after this chicken incident, IPapa came in and made the announcement that something was getting the chickens. Those pesky coyotes were getting too brave. A few days later he came in again and made the statement that he had found a bunch of feathers up the ditch where the coyotes had no doubt dragged them.

Another time the two boys and their cousin, who was spending a few days with us, hiked out to the railroad tracks that ran down through the valley. A small freight train served the three communities south of town.

They hiked over to the old railroad station and up the tracks where the two older boys proceeded to carry out a plan they had hatched up the day before. Horace and his cousin Charles decided to tie Art to the tracks and give him a good scare. Horace had stuck a rope in his pocket, and he told Art this was punishment for tattling on them earlier. They tied Art to the tracks.

It was a good thing that the train had to slow down to a crawl for the sharp turn farther up the tracks for all of a sudden, the boys heard the whistle as the train came to a crossing just before the bend. Immediately, they tried to untie Art but in their haste they couldn't get the knots undone. Art was crying by now, and while their cousin continued to try to untie him, Horace went running up the tracks waving his arms and yelling for the engineer to stop. About that time, the engineer and fireman both spotted the boys, and they applied the brakes. It was a good thing that they had to slow to a crawl coming around the bend for they were able to jerk to a stop just short of Art. They climbed down from the cab, untied him, and then gave the two older boys "holy hell" for their prank.

It was a solemn threesome that headed back to the farm again. Art was sobbing with a pair of wet britches from his scare while the two older boys were alternately hugging and threatening him. They told him if he ever told on them that they would really fix him Needless to say, it was several years before that little episode was told.

As a follow up to the other incident, Horace and cousin Charles talked Art into going out to the tracks again in retaliation for the bawling out that the two older boys had received from the engineer and fireman for their prank of tying Art to the tracks. This time they had swiped a large can of grease from the garage and proceeded to grease the train tracks coming up from the town farther south of them. The train was carrying a heavy load that day, but when it reached the greased tracks, the wheels lost traction, and the train slowly slid back toward the last stop down the valley. Both the engineer and fireman tried to clean off the tracks with some old rags but soon gave up when this did not work. They then brought sand up from the ditch along side and spread this out on the tracks and tried again to get traction for the wheels. The sand worked and they were soon on their way again. They surmised that this had been done by the same kids whom they had so thoroughly chastised a few days earlier. The three boys hiding nearby were extremely satisfied with the results.

Horace was probably the instigator for the greased tracks as a retaliation for the bawling out that they had received for tying Art to the tracks. He usually had no trouble in talking the other two into his schemes. Later, Papa remarked that he could have sworn that he had another can of grease in the garage.

Horace, Evy, Dad, Mary, Art, Frances, and Mom with one more to come.

CHAPTER III

CLASSROOM CAPERS

Now, the boys were certainly no angels at school either. Horace and a classmate of his decided to get even with their teacher one day for an event that had them staying after school again. So, one evening after everyone had gone home, they found a bucket in the small kitchen and filled it with water to take up to the belfry. Here, they turned the bell upside down and filled it with the water. Not being satisfied with this, they proceeded to turn all the desks over and pour water over them as well.

When the teacher arrived the next morning, she was shocked to see the havoc that the boys had wrought in the classroom. She soon decided that she would wait and have the class do the clean-up job, so she headed for the belfry tower room to ring the bell for class. Both of the boys were out in the anteroom to watch what happened. Soon, they heard a loud shriek, and the teacher came running out looking like a drowned rat. The boys ducked back in a hurry, holding their sides to keep from laughing.

There was hell to pay for that one as the teacher called Papa, who was the head of the school board, and insisted that he come up to the school instantly. When he heard what had happened, he took matters into his own hands and stood in front of the classroom demanding to know who the guilty culprit was. He said that everyone in the school would be detained that evening if the guilty party did not come forward. Well, after a few moments of silence, Horace raised his hand and said, "Dad, I can't tell a lie. I did it." He was then taken home by his father and given a sound whipping for this caper. Then, he was told to walk back up to school again.

Mary was in first grade when this happened. The teacher was so upset that, despite Papa's intervention, she decided to kick both of the boys and Mary, as well as the other boy involved, out of school for the rest of the year.

That meant that they all had to attend classes in Elsinore. The boys would have to ride their bikes up to where they could catch the bus for the grade school as it came around the lake. Horace would ride Mary on the handlebars of his bike and they would ditch their bikes in an orange grove across the street. If papa wasn't too busy, he would drive them to the bus stop and pick them up again after they got back off the bus.

Needless to say, that was the last time we saw that teacher. For the next school year, we had a new one. Our new teacher was a real gem. They must have thrown away the mold on her for she was one in a million.

This new teacher at school was well liked by all the kids. I know we all liked her. She seemed to like kids and took us under her wing, so to speak. She not only taught us our studies, but also good manners, citizenship, and even dancing. From time to time she would make taffy for us in the school kitchen and we would have a taffy pull at recess.

A few years later, when she got to know everyone better, she would take the upper grades up to her cabin at Big Bear for a few days in the summertime. Since our dad had a truck, and he and mom had gotten to be good friends with them, he would help with the transportation and mom with the cooking. Of course, we kids would get to go along too. These were great fun times for all of us. The two older boys stayed home and tended to the chores. By this time, they were both in high school and capable of taking care of things.

The boys would pitch a large tent in the campgrounds down below the cabin while the girls would sleep on the porch in bunk beds and cots.

One day, the teacher said that we were going on a picnic to a small lake not too far from there. We all piled into the truck while Mom and our teacher followed in the car with our lunch. Right after lunch a couple of the fellows and I decided to go for a short hike. I guess we got carried away and went farther than we had planned for when we got back, everyone was gone, leaving us to walk back for our punishment, not that we minded.

The following day, two of the girls decided that if I could do it, they could too, so they set off for a hike around Big Bear Lake, not knowing just how far that would be. They were soon missed, but one of the fellows had overheard them talking about it, so the teacher and two of the boys set out by the car to look for them. They finally found them about a third of the way around the lake, both hot and tired. They said they didn't know why they couldn't go for a hike if I had. They were promptly told that two girls by themselves couldn't do that. It wasn't safe and besides it was too far around the lake.

CHAPTER IV

BOYS WILL BE BOYS

The two boys and their cousin were also into the Halloween tricks as well. On one such night, they decided to play a prank on their widowed uncle, who lived nearby. It was a bright moonlit night and after deciding that he was not home, they set to work dismantling his wagon and carried it, piece by piece, up to the top of a shed in back of the house where they reassembled it with the help of a couple of flashlights. They climbed back down and stood back to admire their handiwork, but just then, their uncle stepped out from the shadows with his shotgun. He said, "Good work, boys, but now I'll have my fun. You can bring it all back down and reassemble it again, and see that you do a good job of it too." He was a tough and crusty geezer, and the boys knew they had better do as he said.

The boys got home late that night and were too tired to think of any more mischief. They did vow that they were not going to pull any more of their pranks on him.

The year before they had used a detour sign that they had confiscated a few weeks earlier to place in the center of the highway below the ranch at a dirt crossroad. The arrow pointed up towards the back hills on this road that wound in and out along the base of the hills, coming to a dead end at a considerable distance from the highway.

There were only two small farms up that way. Of course, the locals would know better than to take this road. But, I felt sorry for the unwary traveler. There was the time when Horace got mad at his brother and got out the shotgun intending to scare him. He took a shot at him from a distance, aiming below his feet. When Art fell down, Horace dropped the gun and started to cry, thinking he had shot his brother. He ran over to find that Art had a few buckshot in his backside but was otherwise okay. They were both scared to death, but Art allowed his brother to pick out the few shots with a pocket knife and to put something on that he had retrieved from the house. All the time Horace was begging his brother not to tell Papa on him. At least it gave Art something to hold over his brother's head, finding the threat to tell worked wonders for him.

This medication that Horace had retrieved from the house to put on the wounds after he had removed the shot was a steady standby of Mom's. I can remember her using it on me before when I had picked up a bad case of poison oak. It was on my neck and had turned into ugly looking sores. This was called "zonite," and it burned like the devil. I had run around the dining room table screaming my head off. I'm sure Art must have been yelling too.

One afternoon, our grandfather, who lived alone a short distance down the valley from us, came over in his horse and buggy as he often did to have Sunday dinner with us. He would tie his trusty steed up to an olive tree and have the boys bring over a bucket of water for the horse.

After dinner, Horace and Art sneaked out the back door, untied old Dobbin, and headed for the driveway, jumping up and down in the buggy and shrieking loudly and laughing their fool heads off, they cracked the whip and went charging down to the highway. Grandpa heard them and stumbled out the front door shouting, "Stop you bloody beggars, or I'll use that whip on you." With a loud shout from Papa, they turned the buggy around at the foot of the driveway and started back up to the house.

Being thoroughly chastised by their father, they tied up the horse and made a hasty retreat before an irate grandpa came out of the yard. That was too much for him, so he decided to head back home where he could enjoy some peace and quiet from that noisy household.

The two older boys were soon in high school. They would catch the school bus that came up the valley taking the kids in to the high school in town. While they were still in grade school, they would give Mary and me a ride. Horace would ride Mary on his handlebars, and Art would ride me. Horace would pinch Mary and tell her to sit still, telling Art to trade with him and let him ride me. But Mary knew how to stop that. She would threaten to tell Papa on him. That always brought favorable results.

In high school, Horace would team up with a pal of his when they were out on a date and drive up the long road towards grandpa's place where they would back up to a bank alongside the road and pull out a clump of brush revealing a cask of wine that grandfather had made and kept in there to keep cool and for his own convenience. They would fill their bottles and then head out for their dates and a night of fun.

Both boys were good at sports, especially baseball. They not only played in high school but also in an outside league. We would usually go to the games to watch them.

CHAPTER V

COURAGEOUS TOMBOYS

Horace was an above average student in school, but Art didn't care much for his studies, although he was popular with the other students, especially the girls. He would always volunteer for different jobs. One was as a referee for the girls' softball team on which both Mary and I were members. My sister was an outstanding player, but I can't say the same for myself.

Art would ride our bus to the different school games with the team where he had a steady job as umpire. On one such occasion he was behind the plate, and my sister was doing her usual good job as a catcher. This time she must have been a little too close to the plate, for the girl at bat swung hard and hit her in the head. Mary was knocked to the ground and was momentarily unconscious.

I came running in from the outfield and Art was leaning over her and yelling for a doctor. As I reached them, one of the girls on the opposing team addressed my brother, "What's wrong, sweetie, did your girlfiiend get knocked out?". With this, I yelled at her, "What's wrong with you, he's our brother, you do-do? She could really be hurt."

Mary regained consciousness in a few minutes but had to sit on the bench for the rest of the game. She insisted that she was all right, but she did have a heck of a headache for the rest of the day.

Softball wasn't my sport. I preferred track and basketball. When I reached high school, someone had decided that track was too strenuous for the girls, so they did away with it. That really upset me as I was quite good at it, and I was sure it didn't hurt me or the rest of the gals. Sports were up my alley for I had always been a tomboy while growing up. I felt as though I had been cheated on that score.

Mary and I were together on the basketball team as well as the softball team. Now Evy was quite demure and just wanted to be liked. As for Mary, she was independant with a desire to run everything and everybody. We had dubbed her "bossy cow" when we were young. She also insisted that from then on we would call Papa, "Dad," and didn't hesitate to correct us if we didn't. She said that "Papa" sounded too childish.

It's funny how children can be so very different growing up with the same parents and in the same environment for we were so very different with such different personalities.

Just before one Christmas when we girls were still quite young, our mom brought out a Sears-Roebuck catalogue and asked each of us to pick out a doll that we liked. Evy chose one that was a baby-doll with short curly hair and dimples while Mary picked out one that looked tall and slim and was dressed to the "T's." As for myself, I just said that I didn't want a doll. My mother said, "Of course you do. Just pick out one that you like." I looked them all over and finally decided that the one named Rosemary with long dark hair might not be half-bad.

Come Christmas morning, I remembered there were three dolls under the tree but no Rosemary. When mom asked me why I didn't get my doll, I said "She's not mine, that belongs to Evy." Soon realizing that mom was upset, I picked up the doll and then kissed mom, but that poor doll was an orphan from then on.

My sisters, especially Evy, would sew clothes for their dolls, but I liked nothing better than to call the dog, Buster, and go out hiking towards the low hills to the east behind the ranch.

Now this was rattlesnake country, so the dog was a welcome companion on my numerous hikes. He seemed to know when I was headed for the hills, and he was right there besides me. I'm sure that he enjoyed it as much as I did. If and when we came across a rattlesnake, he seemed to sense it. He was always a few steps ahead, and when he spotted one, he would come to a stop and sort of point with his nose forward and his tail straight out in back. I would then walk around him—both of us keeping our distance. I never did stop to kill one, figuring they had as much right to live as I did.

Speaking of snakes, I was never comfortable with them. They looked too slimy, but Mary, on the other hand, would catch a gopher snake by the tail and call out to our aunt "Look what I've got." At this, my aunt, who was deathly afraid of snakes, would let out a scream and run for the house.

Once, when I was out walking with the dog, he suddenly stopped as we came over a low hill, blocking my way and pressed up tightly against me, emitting a low growl. His hair was actually standing on end. I followed his stare to a ditch down below us to where I could see these two animals eating on the carcass of a dead horse that had been dumped there. They both spotted us and stood silently watching. One thing was sure– neither of us was about to move.

In all my hikes back that way I had never seen them before. They had bobbed tails and short pointed ears and were a mottled tan in color. I had guessed that they were probably bobcats, a male and a female.

They slowly rose from the ditch and headed for the field down below the one that I had intended to follow down towards the house. When they reached the tall grain they would leap up every once in a while to get their bearings.

I started for the dividing fence on the adjoining field and slowly walked down toward the house. I knew that those cats were out there close by. It wasn't necessary to tell Buster to stay as he wasn't about to leave my side. I hugged the fence because the grain on both sides was quite high. The dog and I slowly walked towards the barn down below. The last time I caught sight of those cats they were headed our way, so it was an anxious few moments until we reached the back fence surrounding the horse pasture. We broke then and lit out for the house. That was one hike that I didn't want to repeat. I don't think Buster would either.

Another touchy hike was back up the far ditch towards the hills. I could hear someone shooting and all of a sudden there was a whistling sound close to me, and I knew that they had shot in my direction. I could see two men at the base of the hills and heard them talking, so I let out a yell that there was someone below them. After a brief pause, one of the men called back that they would hold up on the shooting, and the other one said, "Come on up, sweetie." All of a sudden I told myself, "You fool, get out of there," so with the dog right beside me, I rapidly retreated to the house.

Both Mary and Evy were quite happy to be with friends. They had what they called "best friends." I was sort of a loner, though I did have a friend, Nelda, who was inthe same class at school. She would sleep over on occasión, or else I would stay up at her house. Their place was up against the range of mountains to the west. One thing that I didn't like was the fact that they had no indoor bathrooms. You had to settle for the well-known "out-house." That fact didn't bother me too much, not like a couple of "out-house keepers"—two large and ornery geese. They seemed to have my number, for whenever I headed out that way they were waiting for me. It was like running the gauntlet. I didn't know that geese could run so fast. They managed to nip my heels going and coming. I just know that her folks were getting a kick out of each incident.

One day, while staying up there, Nelda and I decided to hike up into the mountains. As we started up from the house she explained to me that they had a bee apiary at the foot of the mountains, but not to worry, for if the bees should take after us to just jump into the middle of the first bush we came to and they'd leave us, that they didn't like cloudy weather or the dog. Of course, it happened to be cloudy, and their dog was with us.

Those critters seemed angry, and as we started through the apiary, they swarmed after us. It was a scary moment as you could hear the loud buzzing and the whirring of all those wings.

I did as she had told me and dived into the middle of a large creosote bush, but she panicked and the last time I saw her, she was running as fast as she could back down to the house.

As soon as it seemed safe, I crawled out of the scrub, circled the apiary and ran down to the house to see if she was all right. My friend had been stung eight times on her head and a couple times on the arm. When I entered the kitchen, she was seated on a stool and both of her parents were slowly removing stingers from her head. Her father said he was about to come up to the apiary to see if I was all right. Boy, she was one sick gal for awhile.

Once in a while, we would get into a tennis game with Jack, the kid across the street from them, who was a grade ahead of us in school. The tennis court was on hard packed dirt, but quite playable.

Jack would at times come down to the house with his father, who liked playing cards or talking politics with our dad. Whenever he showed up, we three girls and Jack would head for the end of the cow's pasture to play tag in this large eucalyptus tree. It wasn't shaped like the rest of the trees that were in a row, but had large branches that spread out not like the usual tall and skinny species.

My sisters were a little timid when it came to swinging through the tree, but Jack and I would make up for it. I guess we were playing *Tarzan*, thinking nothing of swinging from one limb to another. On one such occasion I missed the limb and started to fall. I could hear Evy let out a screem; but I was lucky to be able to grab another branch on the way down and slide easily to the ground.

We also had a tag game in the barn. We could hold on to the 2x4s and scoot along the inside of the barn to escape or jump to a strategically placed pile of hay. We would also climb out the back window and up to the sloping roof where we could drop into the cow's pasture and back in again through the side window.

I remember when I climbed another tree, a large old pepperwood in the back yard. This time I felt a little brave and decided to climb to the top of it. It was slow going, but I managed to make it up, then thought I had better wait a minute or two as our usual afternoon wind came up suddenly. The top of the tree was swaying, and it wasn't going to be easy even without the wind. My sisters were on the ground waiting for me to come back down as soon as the wind let up. Evy soon ran in the house to get Mom. She came out and was wringing her hands and cautioning me to be careful. I told her not to worry that I would make it down soon when the wind wasn't blowing so hard. At that I must have spent close to an hour before there was a momentary lull, and then I came sliding safely back down.

Remembering climbing reminds me of our escapades at school. There were several of those tall spruce and cypress trees in the school yard. It was more of a fellows' game, but some of the girls joined in one where we would swing off the top of the restrooms by grabbing hold of a large branch that we could reach and then swinging out and dropping down to the ground below. Mary decided to try it one day, and as she stood there trying to get enough nerve to jump off, I got impatient as it was my turn next, so I told her to hang on tight, and then, I pushed her off. She made it down okay, but, needless to say, was extremely peeved at me.

Another venture to do with climbing was definitely more risky. This one kid selected one of the tall cypress trees at the end of the playground as a likely tree for his next adventure, and proceeded to climb to the top. There, he clung to a top branch and started sliding down, grabbing another branch as he lost the one that he was holding on to.

We stood there holding our breath, but happily he made it safely down to the ground. Of course I had to try that one too. It sure looked scary from the top but I didn't want to chicken out in front of everyone, so I took a deep breath and started down; luckily, I made it safely to the ground as well. No one else would try it, and once was enough for us as it was far too risky.

Our school track meets were always a lot of fun. There were five schools in our league, and we would travel to the different schools to compete. Several of the parents from the participating towns would also attend as well as those from the communities where the event was held, so we always had a good rooting section. Our school was quite good at the games, and we won more than our share of the ribbons. We would practice for weeks for these games, and since the girls would compete against the boys in our school, we all did well. I know I got my share of ribbons and then some. We would compete in the dash, three-legged race, high jump, relay, obstacle course, distance throw, and in the distance run.

At one of these schools down the valley, I entered the 100 yard dash that turned out most interesting and exciting for me. My brother Art, my strongest supporter, had come along to root for us. Someone told me that one of the girls in the race was really fast and that I would have to go some to beat her. As it was my best event, I thought it would be a cinch. The gun went off, and I realized this gal was right out there with me, so I gave it my best, or at least I thought I had. Then, I heard Art yell out, "Unhitch the trailer, kid. She's gaining on you." I could hear folks on the sidelines cheering as I went all out. I was thinking that she was making a race of it. When I reached the wire, I found out I way-out-run the rest. I heard one of the men say, "Sign her up for the Olympics." My brother came running up about that time and said, "I really lit a fire under you that time, Sis."

As our valley was situated on a small fault line, we were very conscious of the occasional earthquakes. One day, one hit just as I was unloading the wheelbarrow at the back door. I had just leaned over to pick up an armful of wood and ended up falling out of the doorway.

At the same time, Dad had just driven into the driveway and was about to drive into the garage. That car was rocking back and forth like a see-saw. Mary was out near the garage, and she sat right down where she was. We rode through that one with no big problems. I then realized that the kitchen and buffet cabinets in the dining room all had little latches on them, so Mom was well prepared for the shakes.

The animals would all go beserk, trying to hide under machinery or trees. The birds also reacted. They became so very quiet—not a peep out of them.

Birds can be noisy, though. Whenever we heard them talking up a storm, we would know that they were in the fig trees. There were two trees by the lawn in the back yard, and as we were told by our dad that we could shoot them with the twenty-two, Mary and I would get the gun out and see how good our aim was. Of course, we were always supposed to clean the gun afterward, but I usually managed to skip that chore, leaving it mostly to Mary. She was always so conscientious and methodical about it.

There was also an oriole or two to join in with the linnets. These I couldn't shoot as they were such beautiful black and yellow birds. They would build their nests in the palm trees by the driveway where the nests hung down under the fronds, leaving a small hole as an entrance for them.

We all got to be rather good shots. Maybe a little too good for when I spotted a linnet on the electrical wires leading into the house, I took aim at it and shot the wire in two. We had orders after that not to shoot at any birds on the wires.

CHAPTER VI

SUMMER VENTURES

Our summers were always hot, and we would usually go out on the front lawn at night to cool off. We'd throw out a couple of old blankets and lie there watching the stars. It was perfect to star gaze as there were no lights to dim the view. Towards autumn we would count the shooting stars, as we called them. We knew where the big dipper was, the north star, Venus and could see the streak of the milky way stretched out so very clear across the night sky.

There would quite often be flashes of heat lightning off towards the southeast. If by chance it was in our area we had orders to stay down on the blanket.

The start of summer always heralded apricot pitting time. Mary and I would always have a job as our school teacher had a large orchard, and she would hire some of the upper grade students as well as a few from the high school.

Mary was quite good at this. The pitting shed was

out back of the house. Here, we lined up at long tables with a box of cots on one side and a large wooden tray in front of us. The teacher would supervise the girls in the shed while her husband took charge of the boys in the picking and the drying of the fruit.

In one movement, you could half the apricots with a short curved knife, thumb out the pits, and lay the cots on the tray in front of you. We wore tags, and as soon as we finished one box, we got our card punched, and one of the boys would set up another box of cots for us. The fellows would do the picking, keep the tables supplied with the fruit, and remove the full trays to be put into the sulfur tent and then laid out in the sun to dry. The sulfur was to keep bugs out of the dried fruit.

One hot day, the wind shifted, and the sulfur fumes blew back into the pitting shed. I started to feel a bit woozy but kept working. All of a sudden, the teacher came over and slapped me sharply in the face. I didn't know it, but I was about to pass out. She had me sit down and gave me some water to drink. The wind had soon shifted back again, and I was back at work. Everything was run like clock-work. I guess that was a teacher's organization.

This time of year was the Fourth of July holiday and several of the community folks would head for the beach at Oceanside. Someone would go early and reserve space under thatched shade over long picnic tables near the pier. It was sort of a pot-luck affair and a great time for our elders to visit and rest from their busy schedules.

Things were set up and organized by the town for expected crowds. They held track events above the sands of the beach, swimming events, and fireworks from the end of the pier after dark. They would hand out dollar bills for the different track events and for the swimming. I always managed to pick up some pocket money on the races. Mary and I each got a dollar for the three-legged race, and I picked up some for the footraces. They also had one where the fellows would swim out and around the pier and back. Both Art and Horace would enter that one. Horace was quite good at this and would win that event every year. Art always entered, but we would worry until he came struggling back up on the sand again. That was a long and strenuous swim.

The evenings fireworks were outstanding. They shot a few on the end of the pier like giant pinwheels and then so many breathtaking ones up into the sky. At the end, you could hardly see them well through all the smoke from those that were already shot off.

The fireworks were great, but one thing I could have done without were the firecrackers that the boys seemed to enjoy so much by throwing them at my feet. The noise was bad enough, but who wanted to get holes burned in her clothes or have her legs burned?

The beach down there was a familiar place for us as during the hot summer months when Dad was between harvests, he would take Mom and us kids down to a rented cabin by the sand. Mom couldn't stand the hot weather and was in need of a good rest. Little Tommy took a lot of her time when he was a baby as he wasn't doing so well. Dad and the two older boys took care of things at home. Occasionally they would drive down during the day, but they always had to get back to the farm for the evening chores.

Our younger brother, Tommy, had a big problem with eczema when he was a baby. Mom would have to tie his hands down under the covers with huge safety pins to keep him from scratching himself. The doctor had told our folks that he didn't think that he would live, or if he did, he wouldn't have a hair on his head. Mom, believing as she did, told him that he would live and that he would have a head full of blond curly hair. Her words in time proved to be a true conviction.

Once, while we were having dinner, we heard him crying upstairs, and Mom asked me to go up and see if he was all right. It was an awful sight, for he had managed to get his hands loose and had been scratching his head. There was blood all over the sheets and his face and hands. This was supposed to be a hereditary factor, but the folks never knew of anyone else in their families that had had it.

I think that Mom's positive thinking rubbed off on the rest of us for I don't remember any of us going to a doctor. Oh, yes, there was the time that Art had to go to both the doctor and the dentist. When he was a little tyke yet, he had been lying on his back and was tickling one of the work horses on the stomach with an old branch from a tree. That old mare kicked him in the face for his pestering. It knocked out a couple of his teeth, and he ended up in braces for awhile and a partial for the rest of his life.

As for our little brother, he was really spoiled rotten when he was little. I was quite dumbfounded when our dad would get down on his hands and knees and play with him for he had always been so stern and rather dignified. Of course, we all managed to spoil little Tommy. He would throw a fit when he didn't get what he wanted and would lie kicking and screaming on the floor until he turned blue in the face. This usually scared us, but one day when he was having another fit, Dad said, "This has gone far enough. I think he's just spoiled rotten," so he picked him up, turned him over his knee and gave him a good spanking. Then, he put him down and told him that the next time he acted up like that he would spank him even harder. Needless to say, that was the last time he threw another tantrum.

Tommy was pretty much a free spirit for he no sooner got outside then he would throw off all his clothes and run bare-naked all over the place.

Someone had given him a pair of baby ducks for an Easter gift once, and it was hilarious to see him running around the farm with them right at his heels. To them he was "mama duck!" It was a cute picture that Mom captured one day when the ducks had gotten a little bigger with him wearing no clothes holding the two ducks.

As we were growing up, Mom would read to us at night or else recite old stories that her grandmother had told to her. She would also sing us lullabies when we were little. At night, she had us kneel and say a short prayer before we climbed into bed. Even now when things seem to go wrong I catch myself repeating this simple little prayer when I go to bed. I must admit that I do find it most comforting.

As we grew older, it was just natural that we would do a lot of reading on our own. Since our small community had a library on one end of the grocery store, we could walk up and check out our own books. The store was situated at the main crossroads of our community with a post office, a service station, the grade school, and a Methodist church across from the school. We kids were steady members of the congregation there.

My older sister and I would read at night in bed until mom came in and turned out the lights, but this didn't stop us as we had hidden flashlights by the bed and would crawl under the covers and read until we got too sleepy to keep our eyes open.

Sometimes during the day, I would sneak up to our room and crawl out the front window to a gentle slope over the front porch and edge over to a large umbrella tree where I could climb to an overhanging limb and hide amongst the branches and read to my heart's content. It wasn't unusual for me to be missing as I was off hiking with the dog so often.

Evy was always complaining that I didn't take her with me on my hikes, but it wasn't much fun when I did for she talked constantly and was always lagging behind. Of course, I don't think that I would have wanted anyone to go with me.

One day, when she did go with me, we headed up back of the house, and as we came to the hills, we noticed that there were ripe cactus apples all around, so we decided to pick some to take home. We would knock them off with sticks and roll them into our skirts. After we had gathered quite a few, we started back towards the house. Well, if you know anything about cactus stickers you can imagine how far we got before we were itching to beat the band. Those little stickers were all over us, and before long, we were pulling off all of our clothes, piece by piece, and gingerly carrying them as far away from us as we could. As for the apples, they were the first to go.

When we got home, we had to jump in the bath tub where mom had a lot of baking soda, and we scrubbed good with fels naphtha soap while Mom threw our clothes into the washing machine. There was no more attempt to pick cactus apples after that.

There was another time when Evy caught me as I was about to head for the front mountains to pick "Johnny-Jump-Ups" (yellow violets) for mom. They were one of her favorite flowers as they reminded her of her childhood where she grew up on the edge of the Black Forest in Austria. Mary and I had often gone to pick the violets, but this was a first for Evy.

We started out on a dirt road leading towards the foothills by a neighbor's farm to where the violets grew along a dirt roadway at the base of the mountains in the springtime.

We came to a large pasture enclosed by heavy barbed wire where a bull was pastured for breeding purposes. There, I decided to take a shortcut across his domain. My sister was frightened and said, "Oh, no. The bull will get you." Of course this was a challenge, so I slipped between the barbed wire and started out across the field, knowing that Mr. Bull was watching me with his head lowered and pawing the ground. I didn't want my sister to think I was chicken and was hoping that by ignoring his nibs, he in turn would ignore me. Well, I guess that was a challenge to him for he stopped his pawing, lowered his head and came charging after me on a dead run. Needless to say, I didn't play nonchalant anymore, but ran as fast as I could with him hot on my heels. I didn't have time to climb through the fence, so I threw myself on the ground and rolled under it. Evy was screaming by then and I decided to respect old man bull in the future. I was thankful that Buster hadn't gone with us that time, for he might have tried to distract the bull and gotten gored for his efforts.

Evelyn trailed along another time when we headed up the same direction to climb up in the mountains. As we passed our neighbor's farm, the older son was out in the field plowing. He waved as we passed, and we climbed a ways up the mountain to a large rock that projected out and scooted out a ways so we could get a view of the valley. Then, we decided to serenade our neighbors below, so we started singing as loud as we could, "Old man Brown went poop, ploop down the avenue, poop, ploop down the avenue—." We didn't get very far with the song before the fellow plowing in the field down below suddenly called out, "Hey, you kids had better watch out. There are a lot of rattlesnakes up there." We promptly decided to get out of there. We had no idea that our voices would travel so far. I guess they must have echoed off the mountain. We just hoped he didn't stop us on the way back to our place.

These front mountains did have rattlesnakes. They weren't the diamondbacks like in the valley and the back hills, but were sort of a reddish brown in color and were usually larger too.

One day, I did come across a big one when I was running down a fire break from the reservoir in the same mountains where we neighborhood kids would go swimming. This was another mountain rattler, he was stretched out on front of me and as I didn't have time to stop, I just jumped over him and kept on running. I didn't bother to even look back to see if he had coiled to strike or not.

We kids would use the reservoir as our swimming hole. It was perched a short ways up the side of the mountain. We boys and girls would go skinny dipping. When it was the girls' turn one of us would always take turns at being the look-out as we didn't quite trust the boys.

The boys would usually be engrossed in another sport on a steep slope below the reservoir. They had made a dirt track on some hard packed gravel for a run down the hillside. Needless to say, there were a lot of spills and scrapes. They made their own sleds and would name them, having contests to see who could go the farthest.

One of the fellows asked me if I wanted to ride down behind him. He had named his sled "The Strawberry Roan." Thinking that it could be fun, I took him up on it. He said I would have to hang on tight as it would be a bumpy ride to the bottom, and I might fall off the back end, so I wrapped my legs around him and hung on for dear life. I think that the added weight must have made the sled go farther and faster. It was a furious and a bumpy ride to the bottom, but I managed to hang on. He declared a victory for traveling the farthest but they told him it didn't count because there were two of us on the sled. After getting down safely, I decided that once was enough for me. They could keep their sport to themselves. I didn't want to get all banged up like some of them.

One night we were all awakened by a loud explosion. The garage was on fire and was really blazing. It must have started by combustion, possibly by some greasy rags stored next to the car and as a result the gas tank of the car had exploded. Talk of a loud bang! The neighbors must have been awakened by it too; for two of them living not too far from us were over soon to help put out the fire. Dad had pulled on some pants and was down there to move the tractor that was parked next to the garage under a cottonwood tree. This was the roosting place for the turkeys in the summer time; and wouldn't you know it, those dumb birds just sat there and burned to death—this despite the attempt of one of the neighbors to chase them to safety with the help of a garden hose. They did get the fire out without any harm to the other buildings or to the house; but the garage and the car were a total loss.

We three girls and Tommy were down in the entry way by the front door, just in case the house caught fire. Tommy was in the highchair, and we were given orders that we were to stay next to him and not to leave. Mom told us that she would let us know when the fire was out.

I don't think that Dad was too disappointed, though, for he ended up with a new car and garage as well. He liked nothing better than a new car.

As the garage was separated from the chicken coop by a screened area for the chickens, there was no harm done except for a few dead turkeys and a group of hens that had received a good soaking. At least they did have enough sense to huddle in a far comer away from the fire– not like the stupid turkeys in the cottonwood.

The chickens were the mainstay of our diet, not only for the stew pot but for the eggs that they laid as well. Since the roosters were not a priority, they were usually the first to go, leaving just one or two to rule the roost. Now if you haven't been awakened by the crowing of a rooster in the morning, you don't know what you've been missing.

I'll say one thing for them, they really had the harems. Now there was one old biddy that I would like to have thrown rocks at. When one of the roosters was near by, she would run over in front of him and just squat down. I thought that she could at least be coy about it.

On hot summer nights, the older boys and a cousin on an occasional sleep-over would be sleeping on the screened porch upstairs. They would sometimes climb out the window, edge along a ledge on the house, and slide down a large storm drain to the.ground. On moonlit nights, they would soak some old gunny sacks in the cows' trough next to the barn and then swat at the bats that were usually swooping up and down in their quest for bugs. They managed to nail a few of them. It did give the rest of us a good look at what a bat looked like. They were a weird looking lot, sort of hairy things with wings and a sharp beak-like mouth, actually quite ugly.

This escape route from the sleeping porch upstairs was also used by our cousin and Horace to slip out to meet a friend at the foot of the driveway for a night out. At such times, Art wouldn't hesitate to prop a bucket of water over the back door. Then someone would be climbing up the stairs dripping wet.

As Horace and Art grew older, they were a great

help in the fields. The harvesting was sort of a family affair when it came time to bale hay or thresh seed, for Dad's brother and brother-in-law were both there for the field work as they lived close to the ranch.

Both of our uncles lived alone. Dad's sister had passed away not long after she was married, and his older brother's wife had run off with another man, leaving him with three boys to care for. One of the boys had been adopted by his wife's family back in the Midwest, while the youngest had been shot by mistake while deer hunting in the mountains to the west of us when he was quite young yet. The older boy, Charles, shared time at our place and with his father.

CHAPTER VII

TUNED TO SUNRISE

A farmer soon finds out that his time is not his own. It depends on the time of year and on the sun. Today's "daylight savings time" wouldn't apply here. When old Bossy needed milking, it was on her time, and that went for the rest of the farm animals also for they had their own feeding time. The roosters, too, knew when they would give out with their wake-up call in the morning as they were tuned to the sunrise. A farmer soon adapted to their time schedule.

The old bailer and the threshing machines were works of art. Although dusty and well worn, Dad kept them in good working order. He had a small blacksmith shop next to the garden with a forge and several tools and was good at repairing his own farm equipment.

Weather permitting, there were two crops of alfalfa hay and one of oats and barley. It was strictly dry farming and depended on the rains. The rain would either come up from Mexico way or else blow in from the west.

There was a regular routine for harvesting the hay. First, it would be cut, then raked up into piles and allowed to dry before being hauled to a site where the old bailer would turn it into bales of hay that would be stacked in a pile. If the hay was too green, it could cause a fire by a natural combustion.

Dad would cut the hay while the two boys worked at the raking, and after a day or two raked it into hay stacks then picked up and pitchforked into the big "header-bedder" as we called it (that was a high three-sided wagon). One of the boys would ride high in the seat to guide the horses and the other would pitch the hay up into the wagon, changing places occasionally for a much needed rest for the one wielding the pitchfork.

The bailer was hooked up to the tractor by a long belt, and the hay was pitched into an opening where a large wooden arm would tamp it down. As the bales emerged, they were tied with wire, then grabbed by way of two large hooks and dragged to a spot where they were stacked into a large pile. This must have required a great deal of muscle for those bales were heavy.

Dad had several customers who would pick up most of the hay in the field. The rest was hauled to the barn for the farm animals or for future sales.

One day, a gopher snake was accidentally picked up with the loose hay and tossed into the bailer, ending up in the middle of a bale of hay. Dad decided that it wouldn't do as livestock fodder, so the bale was cut open and a battered snake was pitchforked out into the field.

There were large scales down below the spring and the trucks would weigh in before and after loading. Then the customer was charged by the tonnage. These scales were also used by some of the farmers in the valley for a set charge.

In the fall it was close to the same routine with the

seed harvest. It was always a race to beat the fall rains then. Here a seed bag was placed over a chute to catch the oats, wheat, or alfalfa seed. The threshing machine was huge compared to the bailer. It was also run by the tractor. The seed bags were not left out in the field, though, as we had a seed house below the chicken coops. Dad would sell most of the seed and still have a good supply for the chickens and the turkeys.

This was also a busy time for Mom as she would cook the workers a big meal at lunch time. The way that Dad's brother and brother-in-law attacked their food, you wouldn't think that they had eaten for a week. I guess that batching didn't do much for an empty stomach. Of course, it was a light supper for us at night.

Mom was prone to these migraine headaches that really hit her hard. I remember one time when she got down on her hands and knees and begged us kids to be quiet. I felt so very guilty then. Later, I seemed to have inherited that trait from her and knew how she must have felt.

In the fall, after the first rains, Dad would plow the fields that he wanted to plant into grain, and then re-seed them. As for the alfalfa it would come up again from the stubble and would not be necessary to replant for three or four years.

We also had a walnut grove in the upper valley. The older boys and dad would shake the trees with long poles, and we girls would gather the nuts in gunny sacks. This we didn't mind, but we didn't like to hull those that were not open yet, as our hands would become stained a deep brown. As this was the time that we would be heading back to school in the fall, we weren't too happy about it, especially when we entered high school. We'd usually spend a lot of time rubbing our hands in the sand to try to remove the stain.

In the evening, the sacks of nuts were taken home and spread out on wooden trays to dry thoroughly before being resacked. What we didn't keep for ourselves Dad would haul off to be sold by a contractor.

There were also a couple rows of peach trees beside the walnut grove. These we helped pick in the late spring, an itchy job. Peach fuzz will do that to you. You'd need a bath after working all day at that job.

Mom's job would start then, and the peaches would end up in jars that were stacked on the shelves in the cellar. These would be joined by pears and apples as well as cherries from our fruit orchard. We would travel to Beaumont to pick the cherries. With all of us kids, we made out like bandits on that one. We all had our share, eating as well as picking.

The farm was quite productive for we also had cantaloupes and a few watermelons. There was a stretch of land in a low spot down near the road that stayed damp all summer. Those melons were sweet and plentiful. I can remember Dad's picking a gunny sack or two and taking them to a few of the neighbors. Cantaloupes were always a favorite of Dad's, and at the end of the season, he found that if they were placed in a dark cool place in the cellar, they would keep a little longer.

My younger sister, Evy, was a friendly and trusting little girl. One day, when she and I were walking home from school, a stranger in an old beat up car drove up along side of us just as we were about to cut up through the spring to the house, and told us to get in, and he would give us a ride. I said, "Oh, no. We live up here." At that, he said he would take us up to the house as he was going up to see our father. Of course, Evy headed for the car and had the door open before I could stop her. The car was a mess, dirty with torn upholstery, and the man looked just filthy. My sister was pouting because I wouldn't let her ride with him, but I dragged her back and hurried up towards the house with her in tow. I noticed that he had turned into the driveway and up to the house, but he had no sooner got up the driveway then he was coming back down again. As we reached the house, Dad was just coming down from the barn to see who had driven into the yard. I told him what had happened, and he ran for the car and started down to the road to try to catch him. I'm sure he was strong enough to beat the heck out of him if he could have caught him. It wasn't too long before he drove back into the driveway where mom and we two girls were waiting for him. He said there was no trace of him that he just seemed to disappear.

Dad proceeded to tell us that by no means were we to accept rides from a stranger. He stressed the point to Evy, knowing that she was so very much like Mom in the respect that she trusted everyone.

In the summer time, a group of us local kids would head up to the lake to an old abandoned pier and building that was once called "The Showboat," at one time a tourist attraction. This was our adopted swimming spot at the lake. It had been quite plush at one time. There were dressing rooms on the pier; but the whole place was invaded by these huge spiders with cobwebs all over the place; even the boys preferred changing in the willow trees on shore. The only thing wrong with that was those wooly yellow caterpillars that might drop out of a tree onto our heads. There was still an old raft out in the water and that we made good use of.

Summer was a happy and free time for us, no school and all that open place to find something to do or some mischief to get into. If I wasn't out hiking with the dog, I was reading. As for Evy, she was always sewing doll clothes. It was a good experience for her as she was always wearing hand-me-downs from Mary and me. When she got better at her sewing, Mom would encourage her by buying material and patterns. Evy soon became quite adept at making her own clothes. Now, Mom had always sewed for us girls and really knew her job since we were all quite pleased with the outcome.

Evy was the sewer, and Mary must have been the reader. She could go through a book in no time flat. As for myself, I guess I was a dreamer. I did like to make cookies and fool around in the kitchen—that is, when I wasn't out hiking with the dog or reading a book.

One day, when I was sitting on the front steps reading, I heard this racing sound, so I put down the book to see who was speeding down the highway. I knew that someone must be going at an incredible speed. I heard a bang when he hit the dip several yards from the driveway. Then, I saw the car bouncing and that it was on the wrong side of the road and heading for the foot of our driveway. It was obvious that he had lost control of the car, and when he hit the soft dirt at the side of the road, the car flipped end over end and landed upside down in a cloud of dust.

I ran for the fence and with one hand on the fence post jumped over and was running down the driveway. When I reached the car, the wheels were still spinning and a man was just climbing out of the window. I asked him if there was anyone else in the car. He just looked sort of dazed at me and turned around to look back inside the car. I was sure he didn't even know what had happened. About that time, my dad came running down the driveway and seeing me shaking, he told me to go back up to the house and to tell mom to call the police in town.

Well, they drove the man to the doctor's office and had a tow truck haul the car in as well. My dad found a bottle of liquor that the fellow had shoved into the mud of the ditch that ran along the road from the spring. This he turned over to the police who had arrived.

Later, both my dad and I received a subpoena from the court in Riverside to appear as witnesses. I must have been about eleven or twelve at the time and evidently was the only witness to the accident.

When we arrived at the county court house, a man questioned me briefly, nodded his head, and later, I was called to the stand. I know I must have been shaking, and as I looked at the man, I felt sorry for him. I'm sure he must have been really drunk, though. I did say that I was sure he had been speeding, but I wasn't very cooperative, and they didn't keep me long. They had both my dad and the doctor on the stand as well, but neither of them would say much. I do know that he was declared guilty of speeding and drunk driving. After that, I was always conscious of someone going too fast on the highway, for he or she would hit the dip with a bang, and I always wondered if he or she would lose control of the car.

High school was a most enjoyable time for all three of us girls. We were two grades apart, so I was in school at the same time as both of my sisters.

We all managed to make the scholarship society, which pleased our folks no end. Dad was on the school board and was head of it while I was there.

We all had our favorite teachers. I think that mine were Mr. Cass, our English teacher and class mentor, and a teacher we all called "Pop." He was a big favorite of the kids and was my art teacher.

One day in class, this fellow seated in front of me, who would often turn to talk to me, turned around and asked me to go to the show with him that night. As Pop sat up front where we were seated, he could hear and watch us closely. Well, he said to this fellow to turn around or he'd tell his girlfriend on him. He had a steady girl in his same class. Then, Pop just sat there and grinned like a "Cheshire Cat."

About that time, another guy from my class, who was sitting in the back of the room, came up to talk to me and before he could say a word, Pop told him to turn around and go back to his seat. Pop was really grinning now. I guess I really didn't care as the teacher seemed to be enjoying it so much. After class, I told the other fellow to forget it as I wasn't allowed to go out on week nights anyway.

I dated quite a bit in high school but was never serious about anyone. I had made up my mind that I wanted to go on to college. As for my older sister, however, she would like nothing better than to go steady. She did start going with a nice guy when she was a junior, and they became a steady twosome. This seemed to be a status symbol for her.

Mary and I were on the same basketball and softball team. It made it nice to have things in common.

One day, after an intramural basketball game, I was tired and took a little longer in the shower than usual, and got down late to the bus where Carlos, our bus driver, was waiting impatiently to take off. I think he would have left without me, but the kids on the bus were yelling for him to wait. He always waited more or less patiently for the fellows after their games; however, he wasn't so concerned when it came to the girls. My sister and three of the other girls on our team had already climbed aboard.

My fellow riders were cheering when I came running down, and Carlos was off as soon as I reached the bottom steps. To say he was peeved would be putting it mildly.

When I walked back in the bus, my way was blocked

by this kid that I had dated before, so I slid in between him and another fellow, and the two of them managed to do some arm wrestling across the back of the seat behind me.

One day, Mary received a letter from a fellow in the community who had moved recently. She insisted that I read it. I was quite surprised by it. I didn't know that he could be so elegantly romantic. A few days later, I also received a letter from the same fellow. My sister was there when I opened it, and I had to laugh out loud. It was an exact duplicate of the one that he had sent to her. I handed it to her, and when she had read it, she was as mad as a wet hen. She slapped me in the face, but I just laughed at her and walked away.

Grandpa had always been into wine making and Dad decided that he too would try his hand at it. He soon gave up on this and attempted to brew some beer. The first batch that he made blew up on him. It was like rapid gun fire and made a mess of things in the cellar. Mom wasn't very appreciative as she had the shelves full of canned fruit and had a big clean-up job. At least this was the last of his fiascos for he seemed quite satisfied with the result of his next batch and considered himself a good brewer after that.

On those days that the men were into the harvesting, Dad and two or three men would sit out on the back lawn and have a beer or two to cool off. I guess he had mastered the art of brewing for everyone who drank the beer seemed to be thoroughly satisfied with it. At least it put them all in a jovial mood.

When I was a senior in high school, we had our turn at holding a senior stage event in the auditorium. We had planned on having it in the form of a gong show. Several of the kids were to perform, and our class president, who was a good friend of mine, as well as being a most personable fellow, was to act as master of ceremonies. I wouldn't tell anyone what my entry would be, but when I came on stage, no one knew me. I had painted my face black and had padded my clothes and wore a red bandana around my head. I walked up to our M.C. and chucked him under the chin and in a disguised voice told him, "Play Mammy, Sweetie." He drew back as if I had struck him and the audience roared. Some of the band members seemed to know the tune, and I started singing "Mammy," of course, off key. I didn't get far before I got the gong. Just before the gong sounded, I heard Evy cry out, "That's my sister." I think I received the loudest ovation even if I did get the gong. Certainly no one would have expected that of me. I was usually on the quiet side.

While we were still on stage, the school principal came back stage, and I knew that he was looking for me. When he saw who it was, he didn't say anything, but I knew he didn't like it. Of course, the fact that my dad was president of the school board must have had a bearing on the incident.

We only had two blacks in the school. One was a good friend of mine in the senior class. Later, I asked him what he thought of the prank. He laughed and said that he must have laughed louder than the rest of them, especially when he found out that I was the one singing "Mammy."

I had been called into the principal's office twice before. Once was on an editorial that I had written for the school paper that he didn't like and another time when he was trying to get some evidence against this girl that I worked with in the student store. I imagine that she did have her hand in the till as she was in charge of the money and the store. At the time, I just told the principal that I didn't know, but that if he suspected her to confront her about it. Knowing her, I could well imagine that she was guilty.

CHAPTER VIII

GROWING UP

Finally, graduation time rolled around. Mary had already left for Los Angeles and was staying at the YWCA taking a business course at a place called Woodward College. After a year's training there, she ended up with a very good job in the city.

As for both of our older brothers, they were also working in the Los Angeles area. Art had worked in town here at home for a while in a service station, but as he developed an allergic reaction to gasoline in the form of a chronic rash, he had to quit his job, and then he ended up in Los Angeles as a landscaper for a chain of gasoline stations there.

As for Horace, he was working as a salesman for a large food distributor. Knowing him, I'm sure that he would do a good job of it. He was so very good at talking the rest of us into most anything, so I imagine that working as a salesman was a natural for him.

The night that my class graduated it was held in the school auditorium as was the custom. I remember when my name was called when I walked down to where my dad was handing out the diplomas as was his customary job, and when he handed mine to me, I reached over and kissed him, saying, "Thanks, Pop." Of course, that got a laugh and Dad seemed pleased about it. After the services, some of the kids decided to go out and celebrate. They had asked me to go along, but as the folks had asked a couple of neighbors over to celebrate the event, I couldn't very well leave so I went home to celebrate with the old folks. Maybe it was just as well that I didn't go for they were all drinking and our favorite teacher "Pop," who had offered to chaperone the group got drunk and ended up in jail down by the beach.

I knew that Dad had received a phone call early in the morning and took off for the beach city. "Pop" and the kids all got home safely, but that was about all that anyone heard of it. It was pretty much 'hush-hush'. Dad wouldn't give any particulars, even to us.

Now one of the other teachers in school was sure a poor excuse for an instructor. I think he was hired as a coach for sports, but when it came to teaching math he was a "Do-Do." He would ask one of the kids in class, this black friend of mine, who really knew the score to go to the blackboard and diagram the day's assignment and to explain it to the class.

When it was learned that the board had hired someone else to take his place for the next semester, some of the students started to pass out a petition to keep him on the staff. When this fellow who had started all of this asked me to sign, I told him, "No way" that he knew, as well as I did, that he was a lousy teacher. His dad was also on the school board, but this didn't seem to bother him. I never did like this kid and he had always been a thorn in my side. About this time, he approached another classmate who told him off as well. Needless to say, the school board did it their way.

As Tommy, our younger brother, grew older, he fell heir to some of the older boys' chores—one of which was milking the cow. He and Evy were always fighting like cats and dogs. One day while he was milking and she was out gathering the eggs, she crawled through the side window from the barn to retrieve some eggs from a couple of boxes that Dad had nailed over the cows' hay trough since some of those old biddies had insisted on laying their eggs in the manger.

Tommy was usually waiting for her to pick up the eggs, and he would aim the Cow's teat her way and squirt her with milk. She finally had enough of that and started throwing eggs at him. Tommy, being covered with eggs, became infuriated and grabbed a pitch fork that was near by and started after her. Evy dropped her basket and started running. She ran down along the garden to the barbed wire fence, rolled under it and was heading across the stubble field in her bare feet. About that time, Dad came out of the house to go to the barn, and he put a stop to it all, declaring there would be no more squirting of milk or egg throwing. There was only half a bucket of milk that evening as the cow had kicked over the bucket when the eggs came flying that way. There were also fewer eggs than usual.

Tommy had become quite adept at hitting the mark for this one cat, Blacky, was always out there to get her supper. She would sit out a way from him and he, in turn, would squirt some milk her way. He became rather accurate at hitting her open mouth. When she had her fill, she would retreat and wash her face with her paws. Blacky was our favorite of the farm cats. Evy would dress her in doll clothes and push her around in her doll's carriage. The cat would always be docile and cooperative, but she was an excellent mouser as well.

Evy and Tommy would also have a game they played on the roof of the barn. They would climb to the peak and slide down the tin side from the top to see who could slide the farthest. This was on the side of the horse's corral with a high drop off to the ground.

One day, Tommy pushed off extra hard from the top and managed to slide to the edge; but before he could stop he went over and fell down into a pile of dry manure. Being alarmed, Evy rushed down to where he had gone off the roof. When she got there, she found him standing in a pile of the stuff and dusting himself off, smelly but not worse for the wear.

During the summer months, we would often have one or two of our aunt's boys down to spend a week or so with us on the farm. The older one was a little younger than Tommy. My dad had dubbed them. the "Katzenjammer Kids." They would manage to get into a lot of mischief, but weren't nearly as wild as our two older brothers.

There was the time when they were playing with matches out by the barn and set fire to some dry weeds. Dad had to move some of the machinery, and we all pitched in to get the fire out.

Then, they would manage to get something on the farm machinery out of working order while playing at doing the harvesting.

They always had a thing about chasing the turkeys. Those dumb birds would wind up running in circles. At least the boys were running off a lot of steam, and that meant that the rest of us could get a good night's sleep, not the usual laughing and cutting up that would keep us awake.

With those kids, the swallows didn't have a chance. Much like those of the Capistrano Mission, we would also have some of the birds returning here every year. They liked to build their nests in the barn. The birds would build up in the peaks and under the rafters. We always looked forward to seeing them, so Dad soon put a stop to the knocking down of their mud nests. As for food, they had all the bugs they wanted and plenty of mud to build the nests from down in the spring.

Those kids could spend hours down in the spring. They seemed to enjoy catching pollywogs or digging toads out of the muddy banks. The toads they would mark with an "X" on the backs and attempt to find them again the next day.

The spring had been enlarged to a pond at one time by the two older boys who would go up to the lake and catch carp that they in turn brought home and dumped into the pond they had prepared. Mom was quite fond of fish, but as far as I was concerned, she could have them. They were about the boniest fish that I had ever eaten.

As Tommy and his older cousin, Eddie, grew older they would indulge in other amusements more fitting to their age, such as visiting a neighbor who had a couple of girls about their age. This would last until the girls' father sent them "packing" back home again. On one occasion, when the rest of us had gone shopping, they brought the girls back to the ranch with them, telling them that they would teach them how to shoot the gun. They got out the twenty-two and took turns showing the girls how to aim and hold the gun. Of course that meant that they had to put their arms around the girls. The girls seemed to enjoy it as much as the fellows did, but the older one said they had better get home before their dad came looking for them. When their folks found out, they were forbidden to leave home with the boys or to shoot a gun again.

Another time they got inquisitive and went through the dresser drawers in Mary and my bedroom to study our underwear. I guess you could call that the age of puberty for them.

One day, when they went out to the barn to have target practice, they spotted this bobcat lurking nearby in quest of a chicken dinner. That could well have been a decendant of the pair that I had spotted while out hiking that time. They took a shot at him and thought they had wounded him, so they chased him out behind the barn. The cat had gone into the shed in back and had managed to climb up into the threshing machine. The boys thought that he had gotten away, but then they heard this sort of whining noise. It was coming from the thresher, so they crept up slowly and decided that the moaning was coming from inside. Tommy took the gun and slowly climbed up to the top where he could see the cat's stubby tail down inside the opening. He then shot down at him and when they could no longer hear him whining they cautiously grabbed hold of him and dragged him up out of there. Between the two of them, they shoved him off and then shot him one more time to be sure that he was dead.

After that, they both got hold of a leg and dragged him back down to the house to show him off to the rest of us. I'm sure that was one experience that neither of them will ever forget.

The farm seemed to have a strong hold on all of us. Horace and Art would usually come back on weekends and would often bring a friend with them. Art would bring his doctor down once in awhile to go rabbit hunting with him. This rabbit hunting had always been a great sport for the two boys. Sometimes they would go out at night, driving the back roads where they could shoot them by the headlights of the car. I was lucky enough to go with them one time. It was sort of comical, but those rabbits would run into the road in front of the car and stop dead still, making a perfect target. Rabbits were like that. I guess they figured that as long as they didn't move, hunters couldn't see them. That would mean rabbit for dinner the next night. I think we all looked forward to that as it was a welcome change, and we found them quite tasty.

Art was out hunting with this doctor friend of his one day when the doctor spotted a rabbit out near a ditch and started towards it. When he approached the ditch, he came across this rattlesnake. The snake coiled up and started those rattles awhirling. Well, the good doctor took one look, dropped his gun and started running. Art yelled at him to stop. Then, after the snake had crawled back to the ditch, he retrieved the gun, and they headed back to the ranch as this was all the hunting the doctor wanted for that day.

The three of us girls were soon out and on our own too. Mary and Evy both had jobs and I had started Junior College in a place called Ontario. There, I roomed with the same girl that was my friend back in grade school. That dream of a college education went out the window when I met and fell head-over-heels for this fellow from Los Angeles. His father lived just east of Elsinore, so he would frequent the dances in town.

It was funny, but I met him one night at the back gate when he was bringing Mary home after the dance. I was just returning from a date myself. Mary introduced us and made the crazy remark that she guessed that he would be dating me next. Two weeks later, he brought me home, and we went steady after that. He was several years older.

He would drive to Ontario during the week to see me and on the weekends would give Nelda and me a ride home.

Art would be back down on the weekends and would take Mary and me to the dance. We would go together but come home separately. We called these dances the "rat races."

I guess I had it bad. I couldn't wait to get married, so I dropped out of school, and we rode off to Yuma to get married. I was the first of the girls to be married. Both Art and Horace were already married, and it wasn't long before Evy and Mary were also. We were all raising our own families before long. The turn of our younger brother, Tommy, was yet to come.

It wasn't like we had ever left home, though, for we all had a way of drifting back to the farm with our families. Our kids liked nothing better than to go down to the ranch with us. I can remember when our older son got angry at us for being corrected once, and informed us that he was going down to grandma's on the farm. I then offered to fix him a lunch to carry with him but told him it would take him a few days to get there, and he would get awfully cold sleeping out at night in the open. He soon changed his mind and decided he would stay home with us and his baby brother.

All of us would usually congregate at times and would share many a time at the old oak table in the dining room, swapping stories of the past, each telling of his or her own events and experiences while growing up. No one could ever take away those memories. The farm was a mainstay that kept the family together, a source of oneness and belonging for all of us.

I believe that anyone growing up on a farm would agree with me that it would be a memorable experience for all. It's too bad that more kids couldn't enjoy such a memory as this.

Throughout the years we remained a close knit family and were always there for each other.